D1175554

EXTREME SPORTS

MOTOCROSS FREESTYLE

BY THOMAS K. ADAMSON

EPIC

BELLWETHER MEDIA • MINNEAPOLIS, MN

EPIC BOOKS are no ordinary books. They burst with intense action, high-speed heroics, and shadows of the unknown. Are you ready for an Epic adventure?

This edition first published in 2016 by Bellwether Media, Inc.

No part of this publication may be reproduced in whole or in part without written permission of the publisher. For information regarding permission, write to Bellwether Media, Inc., Attention: Permissions Department, 5357 Penn Avenue South, Minneapolis, MN 55419.

Library of Congress Cataloging-in-Publication Data

Adamson, Thomas K., 1970-
  Motocross Freestyle / by Thomas K. Adamson.
    pages cm. – (Epic: Extreme Sports)
  Includes bibliographical references and index.
  Summary: "Engaging images accompany information about motocross freestyle. The combination of high-interest subject matter and light text is intended for students in grades 2 through 7"– Provided by publisher.
  Audience: Age: 7-12.
  ISBN 978-1-62617-275-3 (hardcover: alk. paper)
  1. Motocross–Juvenile literature. 2. ESPN X-Games. I. Title.
  GV1060.12.A377 2016
  796.7'56–dc23

                  2015010406

Printed in the United States of America, North Mankato, MN.

TABLE OF CONTENTS

Backflipping for Gold 4

Motocross Freestyle................ 8

Freestyle Beginnings 12

Motocross Gear 16

The Competition 18

Glossary 22

To Learn More..................... 23

Index................................ 24

WARNING
The tricks shown in this book are performed by professionals. Always wear a helmet and other safety gear when you are on a motorcycle.

BACKFLIPPING FOR GOLD

Taka Higashino launches off a dirt jump. It is his second **run** in the 2013 X Games Motocross Freestyle event. He does a rock solid backflip. He lands smoothly on the ramp.

Higashino continues to pull big **tricks**.
He finishes his run with a kiss of death flip.
His score earns him a gold medal!

MOTOCROSS FREESTYLE

In motocross freestyle, riders do **daredevil** tricks with their motorcycles. Most events include many jumps. However, riders in the Best Trick event only use one jump for their trick.

Other events have a different freestyle focus. Riders in the Best Whip event put their own **style** on the same trick. In the Speed and Style event, riders do tricks while racing.

BEST WHIP
In the X Games Best Whip event, riders take turns flying off the jump. Fans vote for the winner.

MOTOCROSS FREESTYLE TERMS

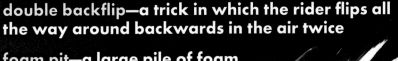

backflip—a trick in which the rider flips all the way around backwards in the air

double backflip—a trick in which the rider flips all the way around backwards in the air twice

foam pit—a large pile of foam pieces that riders land in while they learn new tricks

front flip—a trick in which the rider flips all the way around forwards in the air

kiss of death flip—a trick in which the rider does a handstand on the handlebars while doing a backflip

rock solid backflip—a trick in which the rider lets go of the bike and stays flat in the air while doing a backflip

whip—a trick in which the rider twists the rear of the bike sideways in the air

FREESTYLE BEGINNINGS

In the early 1990s, some motocross riders wanted to do more than race. They started doing tricks as they went off jumps. Fans loved seeing these **stunts**.

FREESTYLE DEBUT
Motocross Freestyle was first an X Games event in 1999.

ON THE FLIP SIDE

People used to think backflips were impossible. Some riders now land double backflips and front flips.

Riders keep trying bigger tricks. Moves that were thought to be impossible have been done. **Innovative** riders continue to excite fans with daring tricks.

MOTOCROSS GEAR

Riders wear colorful **jerseys** and pants. They always wear helmets and gloves. Chest protectors, knee pads, and elbow pads are worn to prevent serious injuries during crashes.

SOFT LANDING

When learning new tricks, freestyle riders practice landing in a foam pit. This keeps them safe when they crash.

THE COMPETITION

For most freestyle events, riders take runs around the course's **steep** jumps. They go for big tricks within a time limit. Each run is scored on its own.

EVENT SCORING

Judges give riders a score out of 100 points. They look for difficult and new tricks. Having many kinds of tricks usually earns more points.

Speed and Style

In the Speed and Style event, two riders go at a time. Each rider gets two scores. They earn points for tricks. The first rider to finish the course gets full points for speed!

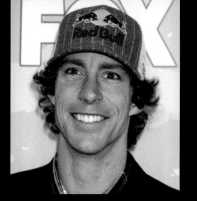

INNOVATOR OF THE SPORT

name: Travis Pastrana

birthdate: October 8, 1983

hometown: Annapolis, Maryland

innovations: Landed the first double backflip in competition in 2006

GLOSSARY

daredevil—risky or daring

innovative—new and inventive

jerseys—shirts with padding to protect riders

run—a turn at competing in an event

steep—almost straight up and down

stunts—acts that show great skill or daring

style—the way something is done

tricks—specific moves in a freestyle motocross event

TO LEARN MORE

AT THE LIBRARY

Cain, Patrick G. *Moto X Freestyle*. Minneapolis, Minn.: Lerner Publications, 2013.

Hudak, Heather C. *MotoX*. New York, N.Y.: Smartbook by Weigl, 2016.

Polydoros, Lori. *Awesome Freestyle Motocross Tricks & Stunts*. Mankato, Minn.: Capstone Press, 2011.

ON THE WEB

Learning more about motocross freestyle is as easy as 1, 2, 3.

1. Go to www.factsurfer.com.

2. Enter "motocross freestyle" into the search box.

3. Click the "Surf" button and you will see a list of related web sites.

With factsurfer.com, finding more information is just a click away.

INDEX

Annapolis, Maryland, 21

Best Trick, 8

Best Whip, 10

course, 18, 20

foam pit, 11, 17

gear, 16

Higashino, Taka, 4, 7

innovator, 21

jumps, 4, 8, 10, 12, 18

Motocross Freestyle
(X Games event), 4, 13

motorcycles, 8

Pastrana, Travis, 21

racing, 10, 12

ramp, 4

run, 4, 7, 18

scoring, 7, 10, 18, 19, 20

speed, 20

Speed and Style, 10, 20

stunts, 12

style, 10

tricks, 4, 7, 8, 10, 11, 12, 14,
15, 17, 18, 19, 20, 21

X Games, 4, 10, 13